In this starkly honest yet poignant collection, Tom Greening shows once again the poetic power of illumination. For Tom unveils for us an intimacy that cannot be matched by theories or scientific reports; his heart and his gut are the investigators, and his pleas, cries, and bemusements are his findings. We may not recognize it at first but Tom is giving voice not just to his own ungraspable trajectory but to the trajectory of every one of us as we age; and to the extent he elucidates that, he gives us all a little more light, a little more compassion, and a little more levity with which to carry on, and sometimes to thrive.

Kirk Schneider, PhD, author of *Awakening to Awe* and *The Depolarizing of America: A Guidebook for Social Healing*

It is with honor and lamentation that I write these words. Dr. Greening once paved the way for me simply by being himself and uttering the phrase "existential shattering." I knew instantly that my life wouldn't ever be the same and that his wisdom lit a torch on a path I would eventually walk. This book, with its beauty, humor, honesty, and frank look at death, will also light a path and lead the way for so many of us who will eventually traverse the path Dr. Greening is currently walking. I imagine that someday, when I reach this point of my life, I will return to this book of poetry to find Dr. Greening, once again, ready to walk me home.

Lisa Vallejos, PhD
President, The Humanitarian Alliance and
Board Chair, Rocky Mountain Humanistic Counseling & Psychological Association

The raw honesty of his slow, struggling walk into the void (death) is a beautiful, yet painful dance between acceptance and rage. Through witty irreverence, sarcasm, and longing appreciation, Tom expresses his fatigue of aging and the feeling of being suspended somewhere between meaningful living with what time remains and being dead without knowing yet know it. The struggle is real. Will you accept his invitation to accompany him, and yourself stare into the void?

Michael Moats, PsyD, Co-Editor, *Capturing Shadows: Poetic Encounters Along the Path of Grief & Loss* and *Our Last Walk: Using Poetry for Grieving and Remembering Our Pets*

From the moment we take our first breath, the Grim Reaper looms, chasing us through life as we desperately maneuver to outwit our finitude—as if death itself is the antithesis of life. *Into the Void* cleverly embraces the vestiges of life as one moves through the processes of aging to in extremis. This book poetically expresses a much-needed antidote to the current fears of dying: It holds the promise of a creative and joyful humanism even till death us do part.

 Nathaniel Granger, Jr., PsyD, Past President, Society for Humanistic
  Psychology (American Psychological Association, Division 32);
Editor, Poetry, Healing, and Growth Series, University Professors Press

As with the ancient and elegant tradition of Jisei, the Japanese Death poem, Tom Greening's collection of verse, *Into the Void,* is a deeply personal farewell to life. Like his earlier works, the poet weaves together pithy observations with heartrending longings for one more day in the light. The practice of Jisei is an effort to show one's mind just as it is, at the very end. This is such a gift from a respected Elder in the lineage of our humanistic psychology tradition, to show us his existential mind, just as it is... near the very end.

           Gina Belton, PhD, Thanatologist
         Psychology faculty at Saybrook University

Into the Void:
An Existential Psychologist Faces Death Through Poetry

by Tom Greening

Colorado Springs, CO
www.universityprofessorspress.com

Copyright © 2020, Tom Greening

Into the Void: An Existential Psychologist Faces Death Through Poetry
by Tom Greening

All rights reserved. No portion of this book may be reproduced, by any process or technique, without the express written consent of the publisher.

ISBN (print): 978-1-939686-70-1
ISBN (ebook): 978-1-939686-71-8

>University Professors Press
>Colorado Springs, CO
>www.universityprofessorspress.com

Cover Design by Laura Ross
Cover Photo Juliet Rohde-Brown

Table of Contents

Introduction by Louis Hoffman	i
Poems	1
My Decline	3
Fix the Faulty Plan	4
I Do Not Plan to Age	5
Grim Poems	6
Let's Fill the Void	7
Aging Jaunt	8
Another Day	9
What Has Become of Me	10
Will God Wake Up?	11
God Chose	12
Nuzzler	13
More Light	14
Challenge	15
Oblivion	16
Sliding Toward Senility	17
Downhill Ride	18
I Manage	19
Old	20
History Proceeds	21
Enseniled	22
Let Me Dawdle	23
Want Help?	24
A Comfy Way	25
Wake Up?	26
My Mundane Story	27
Surf is Up	28
I Flounder	29
Stark Prospects	30
I Dread to Know	31
Eluding Alzheimer	32
I'll Count on You	33
Waning Days	34
Stay Alive?	35

Wangling	36
Denunciation	37
Reverse Time?	38
Objection to Dying	39
Stop Death	40
Bow Out with a Smile	41
When I'm Gone	42
Not Senile Yet	43
What Happened?	44
Lost Battle	45
Poem Fragments	46
Round Up the Poets	47
Clutching at Poetry	48
Poet's Hope	49
Perhaps	50
Aging is Not Fun	51
Aging, Alas	52
Still Grumbling	53
Unexpected Death	54
Defying Fate	55
Grump	56
The Time Has Come	57
I've Not Died Yet	58
Rebel or Fold?	59
What I'll Do	60
Stroke Antidote	61
Hurtling Toward Oblivion	62
Antiquated	63
Fighting Anomie	64
Improve My Fate	65
Loon's Question	66
Where Was I?	67
Let's Not Wait	68
Don't Let Beauty Pass You By	69
Visit Me	70
How I Want to Die	71
About the Author	73

Introduction: Walking into the Void

by Louis Hoffman

Emotions ranging from deep appreciation to profound sadness were ever present as I reflected on what to include in this introduction. Tom Greening has been a friend and colleague for many years, and I knew of his writing, editing, and teaching well before meeting him. Poetry, existential psychology, and dogs were common loves, and our numerous conversations on these topics grew into friendship and professional collaborations. Two of these themes—poetry and existential psychology—come together in this volume (dogs receive more than a few mentions as well). For several years now Tom has been sharing these poems with me, and we have been discussing organizing them into a volume. I am deeply appreciative of Tom's[1] honesty and vulnerability in sharing this portion of his life journey with us. Yet, I cannot deny my sadness as I re-read, organized, and edited these poems, knowing that this last stage of Tom's life is edging toward a close. These poems reminded me of how much I value our friendship and how much I someday will miss my friend.

Into the Void is not an easy read; it is not meant to be. The topic, after all, is facing one's death. Yet, Tom's humor and wit, even when facing the end of his life, soften the blow of the poems without taking away from their honesty. In "Sliding Toward Senility," Tom writes,

> Alas, I now am cruelly forced to see,
> I'm slowly sliding toward senility.
> My valiant windmill-tilting days are past
> and every shallow breath may be my last.

---

[1] With such a personal book, it seemed appropriate to refer to Tom by his first name, not the last name as customary in most writing. It was also important for me, as the author of the Introduction, to use Tom's first name as a way to honor our friendship.

Tom does not shy away from the reality of death or try to distort it through any of the clichés that too often accompany death. Rather, he straightforwardly tells us that he does not want to die.

Along with his angst about his fate, Tom shares some of the comforts that continue to bring him joy. Often, this is where his dog emerges. Tom's current canine companion, Prince, is a dachshund that is largely blind but still a protector of Tom, alerting him to intruders and filling the role of a comforter as they age together. It is his relationship with his dog as well as his human friends that provide him with the most comfort and meaning at this stage of his life. And poetry, too, remains a source of deep contentment and consolation.

Rippling

Irvin Yalom (2009), in his book *Staring at the Sun: Overcoming the Terror of Death*, discusses the concept of *rippling*. He states:

> Rippling refers to the fact that each of us creates—often without our conscious intent or knowledge—concentric circles of influence that may affect others for years, even for generations. That is, the effect we have on other people is in turn passed on to others, much as the ripples in a pond go on and on until they're no longer visible but continuing at a nano level. The idea that we can leave something of ourselves, even beyond our knowing, offers a potent answer to those who claim that meaninglessness inevitably flows from one's finiteness and transiency. (Ch. 4, "Rippling section")

Because rippling often is not intentional, it is easy to miss the impact we have had on others.

In my conversations with Tom in recent years, he often wondered about the impact that he will leave behind. He would voice concern about the future of humanistic and existential psychology as well as some of its more prominent institutions. These were not merely labels for types of psychology and institutions where he served and worked; they were part of him. As for so many drawn to these approaches to psychology, humanistic and existential psychology are *who he is*, not just *what he did*. These are values he believes important for making the world a better place. He does not want to see them or his contributions just fade away.

Last year my two oldest sons and I visited Tom in his long-time home in Sherman Oaks, California. He walked us around his home, telling stories about raising his family there, including fond memories of his wife and daughters. Then he told us stories about the many pictures and artifacts that he maintained around his house. Among these memories were stories about the history of humanistic and existential psychology—a history in which Tom played an important role. He served as the editor of the *Journal of Humansitic Psychology* for over half its lifespan to date, and he is the only living person to have maintained a connection with Saybrook University from its inception through today. He was a founding board member of Saybrook University when it began as the Humansitic Psychology Institute and remains a professor emeritus of the university. When I speak with others about Tom in humanistic and existential psychology circles today, fond memories of Tom quickly emerge. Many contemporary leaders in these movements were students of Tom.

While Tom spent more time and energy helping to develop and promote the scholarship of others, he made important contributions himself. Concepts such as existential shattering (c.f., Hoffman & Vallejos, 2020; Hoxie, 2013; Ren, Gao, Yang, & Qu, 2018; Vallejos, 2015) and existential dues (Claypool, 2010; Hoffman, 2017) originated from Tom. Although he did not write about these topics, conversations with Tom inspired students and colleagues to pursue and develop these important concepts. These are concepts that I use in my work with clients as well, and I have observed the value of Tom's ideas beginning to ripple through them.

Tom's most powerful ripples, though, were undoubtably his relationships. These relationships took many forms—some out of the ordinary. For example, one way that Tom showed his concern for people and for scholarship was through his careful editing. I remember the first time that I served on a dissertation committee with Tom. I had a reputation for being a thorough editor of students' work (sometimes to the dismay of students); however, when Tom reviewed the dissertation, he found many little details that I had missed. As the meeting concluded, we spoke for some time of Tom's careful attention to the content and writing of the dissertation. For students, I am sure it is easy to not recognize the care—and even love—that can be part of such editing. It can feel overwhelming and even critical. But for many professors, close attention is an act of caring. Often, this is not recognized until the ripples have become smaller and the student looks back, recognizing the writer and scholar they have become. In my conversations with Tom, I remember him sharing that he line-edited every paper he received. It was not for enjoyment or criticalness that Tom did this; it was out of a commitment to the author and a commitment to scholarship.

Tom's relational ripples extended far beyond editing. He often gave freely of himself. It was rare that I reached out to Tom when he did not find time to talk. At conferences, I would sit for long periods of time talking with Tom. Unless he was off to see one of his students present, he seemed always willing to give his time to those who wanted to talk with him.

Mentoring is another way Tom's commitment to relationship was evident. At the First Annual Society for Humanistic Psychology Conference, there were only two presentations that involved students; one was a student presenting with Tom. Often, I would hear of Tom boasting of his students' scholarship and contributions well after they graduated. His pride in his students remained evident after their degree was complete. This is one reason why many of his students maintain such reverence for him.

When you dive into a swimming pool, it is often hard to differentiate the ripples created by you crashing through the water from the other ripples and disturbances in the water. But even if we cannot see it, and even if we cannot tell if the impact was from us or some other source, the impact remains. When standing at the side of the pool watching the splash, it is much easier to see the impact of the dive. I am thankful that I was one of the many observers standing poolside as Tom's ripples made their way across the educational swimming pool, touching the lives of many, even when Tom did not recognize the impact.

Humor

Many of Tom's friends and colleagues are quite familiar with Tom's dry, yet poignant humor that often bordered on being irreverent. This can be seen in many of the poems in this volume. At times, the poems simply reveal the wit that serves as the source of Tom's humor. At other times, his humor has a more direct message. However, most of Tom's humor serves to disarm difficult topics. This is the bulk of the humor in *Into the Void*, as well as that of his previous volume, *Words Against the Void* (2017). Death is not easy. The mixture of Tom's witty, dry humor makes the topic more bearable. For example, in "I Flounder," Tom writes,

> I flounder, don't know what to do.
> I fear I may end up like you,

adrift in this vast universe,
a wanderer, a bum, or worse.
Consult my dog? But why do that?
He hardly knows where he is at.

This poem is not one of the more profound poems on death in this volume, but the intermix of humor about the human condition makes it easier to sit with the dreary, angst-filled poems that populate much of the book.

Zhi Mian: To Face Directly

Zhi mian therapy was developed by Xuefu Wang, based upon the writings of the Chinese literary figure, Lu Xun (Dueck & Wei, 2019; Wang, 2011, 2019). This approach to therapy is considered an indigenous Chinese approach to existential therapy. The phrase zhi mian can be translated as "face to face" or "face directly." This is a rich concept that can be interpreted as facing oneself directly (i.e., authenticity), facing others directly (i.e., genuineness), and facing life or the world directly. Being honest about the human condition is a primary value of much of existential thought (Hoffman, 2019).

This volume of poetry provides a powerful embodiment of zhi mian. In many of the poems, Tom unflinchingly faces the harsh realities of death, including his personal facing of mortality as well as the relational dimensions of death. In true existential form, Tom does not offer answers to these solutions, but rather seems to invite us to be similarly honest about our own reality in the face of death. While the poems often seem to beckon the question of meaning in life and in death, they do so without suggesting that there is no meaning or purpose. Rather, Tom recognizes that it is in the struggle that we find the answers. If we are not willing to struggle, then it is unlikely that we will find authentic answers, and it is unlikely we will find the answers that we need. Thus, while the poems in this volume may seem morbid at times, if the reader can hold on to the value of the struggle, these poems provide the reader an opportunity to get closer to their own answers pertaining to meaning and mortality.

Conclusion

Into the Void is a true existential gift. It is not often that we have the opportunity to witness an authentic journey with mortality as one faces his own death. Tom has given this to us. As is the case with any authentic journey, this volume offers an opportunity to laugh and an opportunity to cry. But, most important, it offers an opportunity to reflect on the bigger questions of life.

In one of the recent conversations I had with Tom, he reflected that "Death is part of life, and this paradox should be part of a lively discourse." Certainly, this is a discourse that Tom has enriched greatly with these poems. I am confident that this conversation will continue well after Tom's journey into the void has finished.

Thank you, my friend, for your authenticity, for your legacy, for your friendship, and for your ripples.

References

Claypool, T. (2010). *On becoming an existential psychologist: Journeys of contemporary leaders.* ProQuest, UMI Dissertation Publishing (3412340).

Dueck, A, & Wei, G. Q. (2019). The indigenous psychology of Lu Xun and Xuefu Wang. In L. Hoffman, M. Yang, M. Mansilla, J. Dias, M. Moats, & T. Claypool (Eds.), *Existential psychology East–-West* (Vol. 2; pp. 17–46). University Professors Press.

Greening, T. (2017). *Words against the void* (Rev. & expanded ed.). University Professors Press.

Hoffman, L. (2017). Introduction to *Words against the void* (Rev. & expanded ed.). In T. Greening (author), *Words against the void: Poems by an existential psychologist* (pp. 7–14). University Professors Press.

Hoffman, L. (2019). Introduction to existential–humanistic psychology in a cross-cultural context. In L. Hoffman, M. Yang, F. J. Kaklauskas, A. Chan, & M. Mansilla (Eds.), *Existential psychology East–West* (Vol. 1, Rev. & expanded ed.; pp. 1–72). University Professors Press.

Hoffman, L., & Vallejos, L. (2020). Existential shattering. In D. Leeming (Ed.), *The encyclopedia of psychology and religion* (3rd ed.; pp. 847–850). Advanced online publication. Springer. https://doi.org/10.1007/978-3-642-27771-9_200193-1

Hoxie, E. (2013). *The impact of traumatic brain injury from spouses'/partners' perspectives: Transcending existential shattering* (Order No. 3594257). Available from ProQuest Dissertations & Theses Global. (1442476141).

Ren, Z., Gao, M., Yang, M., & Qu, W. (2018). Personal transformation process of mental health relief workers in Sichuan earthquake. *Journal of Religion and Health, 57,* 2313–2324. https://doi-org.libproxy.uccs.edu/10.1007/s10943-018-0584-4.

Vallejos, L.M. (2015). *Shattered: A heuristic self-search inquiry of one mother's journey to wholeness after a child's diagnosis of a potentially fatal congenital heart defect* (Order No. 3725141). Available from ProQuest Dissertations & Theses Global. (1732168265).

Wang, X. (2019). The symbol of the iron house: From survivalism to existentialism. In L. Hoffman, M. Yang, M. Mansilla, J. Dias, M. Moats, & T. Claypool (Eds.), *Existential psychology East–West* (Vol. 2; pp. 3–15). University Professors Press.

Wang, X. (2011). Zhi mian and existential psychology. *The Humanistic Psychologist, 39,* 240–246. https://doi.org/10.1080/08873267.2011.592465

Yalom, I. D. (2009). *Staring at the sun: Overcoming the terror of death.* Jossey-Bass.

Poems

My Decline

I made a grave mistake and lived too long,
and now I find I am not young and strong.
Instead, I am a tottering old fool
who dozes off and is inclined to drool.
Encyclopedic knowledge once was mine–
I could all sorts of useful things design.
Inventions poured forth from my clever head,
but now it seems my brain is three-fourths dead.
The messed-up universe is going to be
a much worse place when it can't count on me.

Fix the Faulty Plan

I can't conceive of any reason why
we mortals all must age and then we die.
This seems to me a very faulty plan,
unholy and unfair of God to man.
Unless he is a cruel, uncaring dunce,
I'm sure that he will fix this flaw at once.
The lengthy dawdling that we've seen before
can't be condoned– He surely knows the score.
Since "God is Great" he can command a change.
This is a major fix he must arrange.

I Do Not Plan to Age

I do not plan to age at all.
I will not heed that late-life call.
Denial is my stolid stance–
Just watch my death-defying dance.
Three cheers for my longevity,
evasion of senility;
vestigial, partial sanity;
contained, mundane inanity.
While other dolts grow old and die,
I clutch at humor, droll and wry.

Grim Poems

How strange it is that grim poems have a way
of brightening a gloomy, morbid day.
I dwell on them no matter how morose,
and crave a strong and nearly lethal dose.
Don't make me laugh–I cannot stand the pain.
From humor there is nothing one can gain.
Don't let some corny, cheerful Hallmark card
delude you that life's anything but hard.
Just give me dreary, bleak, and downcast views–
that is the stuff my starving soul renews.

Let's Fill the Void

Let's fill the void with fertile emptiness,
rake in blank space, pile up a vacant mess.
It's nada that we pilgrims truly need–
naught else can satisfy our boundless greed.
Of course we know this really makes no sense,
and God will offer paltry recompense,
but frantic fulmination is the way
to keep the threat of rectitude at bay.
If ludicrous all this fine madness seems,
go back to having normal, boring dreams.

Aging Jaunt

This aging jaunt is overrated.
Its merits should be more debated.
Enrichment, joy? A glaring lack–
I'd like to get my money back.
Though youth can sometimes hit a snag,
old age is just an endless drag.
I'd pay a fortune to retrieve
some truths in which I could believe,
but farthings are in short supply,
and so, alas, quite blind I'll die.

Another Day

I'm facing yet another day,
but cannot seem to find a way
to rise up from my comfy bed
and show the world I am not dead.
I lie here snug, the dog and I,
and look for signs I did not die,
but I admit they're faint and few
and mostly my poor brain's askew.
There's so much in my life I rue--
I wish I were as wise as you.

What Has Become of Me?

Some old pals asked what has become of me.
I sit for hours in pensive reverie
and transcribe poems my dog bestows on me,
pathetic victim of insanity.
For years I ably fought senility,
but now this dismal fate creeps up on me.
I gulp some pretty pink and yellow pills
alleged to cure my esoteric ills.
My dog demurs and says I ought to spend
more time in petting him, my truest friend.

Will God Wake Up?

What bumbling fool designed the human race?
Who thrust into the world this sad disgrace?
Some amateur who never had before
concerned himself with how to prevent war?
So here we are, stuck in this mortal realm,
with trolls and devils fighting for the helm.
Will God wake up and see what he has done
and not just foist this off on his poor son?
As eons pass the answer is less clear.
I fear the end of time is growing near.

God Chose

I did not want to age and die.
I saw no valid reason why
I should submit to such a fate.
My remonstrations came too late.
It turned out God had his own plan
to make me just a mortal man.
Aloof, he never queried me
on what I'd like my fate to be.
He simply went ahead and chose
his way my sinecure to close.

Nuzzler

Each day I waken glad to see
my dog intent to nuzzle me.
Now as I age my prospects dim
and I depend still more on him.
Most elder friends have passed me by;
on cats for sure one can't rely,
so I give thanks before I die
I have this dog who helps defy
incursions from mortality
with early morning coquetry.

More Light

As aging steadily proceeds
the shoreline of my life recedes.
Some happy times I still recall,
but others fade behind a pall.
My mind meanders, stumbles, fades,
gets lost in murky everglades.
Now growing gloom portends my end
around the next endarkened bend
and I'm condemned to Goethe's plight,
beseeching you for still "more light."

Challenge

A challenge I am loathe to face:
How can I now decline with grace;
how best shrug off this mortal coil,
no longer as an earthling toil?
I live each day resentfully,
as fate inflicts its woes on me.
I'd rather sail quite merrily
to paradise beyond the sea,
or zoom up into outer space,
in paradise assume my place.

Oblivion

My days on earth are nearly done.
Next resting place? Oblivion.
The ambiance is cool, I hear,
and residents need never fear
eviction or some noisy crowd–
loud revelry is not allowed.
Amidst such peace I'll vegetate
and my great virtues contemplate.
No longer by cruel conscience run,
perhaps I'll even risk some fun.

Sliding Toward Senility

Alas, I now am cruelly forced to see,
I'm slowly sliding toward senility.
My valiant windmill-tilting days are past
and every shallow breath may be my last.
Diminished daily by eroding age,
I am reduced to helpless, fuming rage.
As muscles cramp and weak synapses stall,
I live in constant fear that I will fall.
I sputter protests no one cares to heed.
Where is the magic potion that I need?

Downhill Ride

The aging process is a downhill ride,
a bumpy one I barely can abide.
My body doesn't function well–a loss.
It does not recognize who is its boss.
More pressure only serves to make it balk;
it stumbles when I try to take a walk.
Loud exhortations fail to motivate
this creature whom I've lately grown to hate.
I will replace it soon if I can find
a docile one who will obey my mind.

I Manage

I am not yet depressed and dying,
although some enemies are trying
to portray me as nearly done,
incapable of joy or fun.
I may fall in an awful slump
and mope about like some grim grump,
but soon I will cheer up again
and manage to appear half sane,
perhaps a little worse for wear,
but in no danger of despair.

Old

I like pretending I am young,
but my old brain has got unsprung.
It rattles when I cough or sneeze—
I fear I have some dread disease.
Synapses falter and burn out–
I'm left with morbid angst and doubt.
Hashish can help me through the night,
but hardly makes me erudite.
For guidance may I turn to you,
or has old age besieged you too?

History Proceeds

As I grow old, I note that history
proceeds apace without much help from me.
I'd intervene, but don't expect to see
in this long tale much but more tragedy.
What could I do to stem this tide of woe?
I fear that's something I will never know.
I'll soon be gone; more dramas will ensue.
The happy ones will always be too few.
It's clear that none of this upsets my dog
who, as I write this, slumbers like a log.

Enseniled

I'm just an old enseniled man
who crambles by as best he can.
My education was quite brief–
I learned the hard way: Time's a thief.
Those French guys were so very smart:
Rousseau and Proust, Camus and Sartre.
Verlaine and Denis Diderot,
that freaky poet Paul Rimbaud.
Now they're all gone, and who'll replace
such founts of wisdom for our race?
I think you can quite clearly see
it will not be a dolt like me.

Let Me Dawdle

I hope that I will someday be
content with my senility,
not always churning in revolt,
and crying loudly, "oy gevalt."
Just give me chicken soup and bread–
I want to slumber late in bed.
Turn off the lights, the TV news,
and let me dawdle, snore, and snooze.
The world won't get much worse too fast,
and I deserve some peace at last.

Want Help?

It's quiet here and deathly still,
and though I am not poor or ill,
all day I have been petrified,
and sought assurance I've not died.
My ditsy dog declines to help–
I get no solace from his yelp.
My courage now is worn quite thin,
and thus the anxious state I'm in.
Some faint meows come from the cat–
I'd like to know, what help is that?

A Comfy Way

Life may be harsh, but not for me–
I've found a comfy way to be.
I am adept at fantasy
and flee from gross reality.
I sleep a lot and hide in dreams,
then conjure up ambitious schemes.
I strategize great victories
and dodge around unpleasantries.
I swig a nip and close my eyes,
assure myself I'm brilliant, wise.

Wake Up?

I'd like to show some love before I die,
to do a little good, and so I'll try
and beg and pray that I may have the luck
to mend my ways, stop being such a schmuck.
In times gone by I never thought of this–
my selfish enterprises went amiss.
I wondered why life seemed such an odious chore,
deficient in some basic core.
Can I wake up while still there is some time
and remedy this existential crime?

My Mundane Story

My mundane story slowly now winds down,
and I've accomplished little of renown.
No sturm und drang, no great festivities,
a few good deeds, some corny levities.
At least, I claim, I have not been a troll.
I plied some humor, attempting to be droll.
My dog's well fed and never snaps at me.
I marvel at my blooming orange tree.
I hope I'll find a way to gracefully
depart this realm with no indignity.

Surf is Up

I'm going to liven up and have some fun;
I'll not concede that I am finished, done.
This winter I will ski an alp or two,
catch some gazelles and give them to the zoo.
I'll climb a tree and grab an eagle's feet,
then soar through clouds until I land in Crete.
I'll show the world the vigor I've still got
by single-handling my resplendent yacht.
The surf is up, my narcissism too.
You'll see: There is a lot I still can do.

I Flounder

I flounder, don't know what to do.
I fear I may end up like you,
adrift in this vast universe,
a wanderer, a bum, or worse.
Consult my dog? But why do that?
He hardly knows where he is at.
Seek out a psychic? Plan a crime?
I might just end up doing time.
My thinking is not very deep,
so I will just go back to sleep.

Stark Prospects

I do not say my prayers every day,
and thus from God have drifted far away.
He's busy with more urgent things to do
than fret about such dolts as me and you.
So on I grope, confused and in the dark–
my earthly prospects ever grow more stark.
Redemption seems unlikely at my age–
I must keep braced for some new horrid stage.
I fear I will be captured by vile gnomes
and forced to read and memorize my poems.

I Dread to Know

I trim my hedges twice a day.
It's thus I waste scarce time away.
The papers on my desk, in turn,
await my choice to shred or burn.
To raise the odds I'll stay alive
I wash the car but never drive.
The dog has promised not to die
until, like angels, I can fly.
I dread to know what time I've got.
Eternity? Most likely not.

Eluding Alzheimer

Doc Alzheimer is stalking me
to steal my precious memory.
I will elude him–you will see
how I can dodge quite cleverly.
I hide my thoughts deep in my head
and act like I am dumb instead.
This fools that evil, scheming thief
and saves me lots of stress and grief.
I seldom think these days at all...
at least as far as I recall.

I'll Count on You

I'm finding life is too much trouble.
Please put me in some kind of bubble
where I at last will safely be
immune to life's depravity.
Shut out the world, stop all the stress,
indulge my wish for happiness.
Install me on a fluffy cloud
where aggravation's not allowed.
I'll count on you to guarantee
I'll live in pure tranquility.

Waning Days

The callous clock consumes my waning days.
They vanish in an all-consuming blaze.
I'm left with ashes and some memories
soon scattered by the slightest callous breeze.
Will ashes ever turn to shiny gold?
Not in this blighted lifetime, I've been told.
They lie amongst decaying fallen logs,
in swamps, vile pools, or fetid shadowed bogs.
Will some new god restore what's blown away?
May I have hope I'll see that wondrous day?

Stay Alive?

My friend has ordered me to stay alive.
How does she think I can this feat contrive,
and do it in a storm-tossed lethal realm
with such a drunken demon at the helm?
Let her keep living if she wants to try.
Some weary pilgrims just give up and die.
But as for me, I plan to hope, not waver,
fight off my quivering and quaver,
endure a while to see what may unfold,
and pray that dross next year will turn to gold.

Wangling

My fleeting days on earth are nearly done.
I've had some love, some laughs, and lots of fun.
While looking back, what do I want to say?
What do I wish I'd done some other way?
Replay the reel a thousand scenes or more.
Delete the ones in which I'm such a bore.
The cruel acts I grievously regret–
Their memory dwells in my conscience yet.
But overall this epic may suffice
to wangle me a spot in paradise.

Denunciation

I want two legs that really work,
not ones like mine that spasm, jerk.
I want a lucid, clever brain,
not one so flawed and prone to strain.
I'd like to speak coherently
and not display my lunacy.
My dog can growl and bark with ease,
but I just sputter, gag, and wheeze.
I must chastise, denounce, malign
the gods for causing my decline.

Reverse Time?

The days grow short and I get older
while I just sit around and molder
and make up new ways to complain
about each minor ache and pain.
There's nothing useful that I do
and so I idly fuss and stew.
Another year will pass me by–
before too long I'll surely die,
unless, of course, by writing verse
I can the flow of time reverse.

Objection to Dying

I won't object to being dead,
but getting there is what I dread.
Who deemed that dying be required?
A God like that should be retired.
The process is a downer and
too much about it I can't stand.
I'd rather take a final cruise,
or drift into a pleasant snooze.
Get back to me when you revise
the final plan for my demise.

Stop Death

Death is a scourge that must be stopped.
Too many normal, decent, innocent people
are felled by it annually.
Sadly, routine and necessary activities,
such as eating, breathing, sleeping,
have been identified as precursors.
Most people who engage in sex
fail to achieve immortality.
Even cautious sedentary hobbyists
such as stamp collectors, weavers
and knitters often succumb.
Gardeners routinely die,
occasionally in their gardens.
Most robust Olympic athletes have died.
Cooks have died after eating their own meals.
Strong, life-affirming people
nevertheless have a high rate of death
if their parents or siblings died.
A movement titled "Deny Death,"
described in a book by that name,
flourished in the crazy 1960s
but faded out,
and most of its adherents died.
My advice: Deny or avoid death
if you can, or delay it
as long as possible.
When it comes for you,
don't give your right name.

Bow Out with a Smile

All mortal men must someday say goodbye,
but I'm still here for no good reason why.
One's term on earth–it may be long or brief;
death be a curse or a desired relief.
Make your complaint–you'll get a smug retort.
The fates don't care–they play with us for sport.
I've seen my friends live long or short, then die.
Don't waste your breath, don't uselessly decry
how fast your borrowed tenure here goes by,
how rapidly your certain end grows nigh.
Be grateful that you got to last a while,
then bow out with a gallant wave and smile.

When I'm Gone

I'm blessed because my life is seldom hard.
I have a verdant garden and big yard,
a loving dog and dedicated friends,
fair old-age health that somehow never ends,
no warning signs of virulent disease,
three thriving children and their families.
But in the troubled world surrounding me
I see much dire unfolding tragedy.
I read of wars, wish I could intervene,
of deserts that I wish I could make green.
Soon I'll be gone, and all will be the same,
much like it was before to earth I came.

Not Senile Yet

There is a lot that I forget,
but senile I am not...just yet.
My mind sometimes abandons me
or drowns me in cacophony.
Synapses sputter, fray, and die,
no longer am I young and spry,
but this I surely will remember:
my birthday's coming in November.
I hope that then I still will be
secure in immortality.

What Happened?

Long years ago I had a life–
a job, two children, and a wife,
a dog, a house, a verdant yard,
some worthwhile work that was not hard.
Most citizens obeyed the rules;
my nation was not run by fools.
My dog had fleas, but very few;
the government knew what to do.
What happened? Seems like overnight
all sanity has taken flight.

Lost Battle

I want to sleep, not be awake.
There's only so much I can take.
I find that stark reality
persists in overwhelming me.
For years I tried to cope with it–
I lost the battle bit by bit.
Sobriety worked not at all.
I failed at drugs and alcohol.
I've given up on consciousness–
it turned my brain into a mess.
Please help me find another way
to get through yet another day.

Poem Fragments

I am an empty old shell of a man
at whom during the night
an occasional poem fragment
is wafted or hurled.
I keep pen and paper at my bedside
to catch it with scribbles,
and it awaits my incomprehension
in the befuddled morning.
Why not just sleep?
These poems fill paper,
but not me
or the hungry world.

Round Up the Poets

The lifespan of a poem is often very short.
Some get dismissed with just a sneer or snort.
That is the way that it should always be–
The world should not be cursed with poetry.
To best contribute to our common good
it's obvious to me that all of you should
round up the poets, throw them off a cliff.
Do not demur, and never question if
there's one amongst them who is slightly sane–
A search for him would surely be in vain.

Clutching at Poetry

I dwell on things I cannot do–
the things I can are growing few.
The bills pile up, the dog has fleas,
my roses have some rare disease.
My pool is dirty, growing scum.
I wonder–will the pool man come?
Abandon ship? I am not ready,
though I grow weary and unsteady.
This aging is defeating me,
and so I clutch at poetry.

Poet's Hope

It very soon will be my time to die.
How will I make these fleeting days go by?
I'll write more poems, then wonder who will read
such scribbling, but I vainly crave and need
a faith, delusion–call it what you will–
that they amount to something more than swill.
No classic verses will you get from me,
but some, I hope, read entertainingly.
The rest of them perhaps you'd like to save
and throw on me when I am in my grave.

Perhaps

I found myself sad, lonely, half alive,
and wondered how I might somehow survive,
then also asked the haunting question, "Why?"
From nowhere came this blunt and terse reply:
"Because I will it, and you're simply stuck,
condemned to wallow in life's dreck and muck."
What could I do? I went about my day,
made vain attempts to cheer up and to pray.
By evening I'd managed to persist,
and now, today, perhaps I still exist.

Aging is Not Fun

My slow descent into senility
I must proclaim does not appeal to me.
I think I can speak out for everyone
when I assert that aging is not fun.
Few pastimes are so morbid, grim, not droll
as facing that you're just a mortal soul.
I'd rather take a fancy cruise instead,
but not with somber shipmates all half dead.
Is there a kindly host who will provide
a haven where no one has ever died?
Please get me there by plane or train or boat–
A place like that will surely win my vote.

Aging, Alas

Alas, my mind is growing dim and slow.
I can't recall so much I used to know.
Instead it gets invaded constantly
with sheer superfluous inanity.
I still write poems, but am less good at that,
and can't remember where I left my hat.
I'd lose my head were it not well attached;
my socks are often dirty and unmatched.
The dog must tell me when it's time to eat–
I fear this aging process has me beat.

Still Grumbling

Arising to one more depressing day,
still stumbling, grumbling, bungling on my way,
a wobbly wanderer, a downcast, doleful fool,
complaining that the fates are harsh and cruel.
I sulk, my life is dismal and morose,
I bristle if some well-wishers get close.
Lugubrious and gloomy–that's my style.
I long ago gave up attempts to smile.
Now here you come with saccharine goodwill–
it is enough to make me still more ill.

Unexpected Death

One newspaper described his death
as "unexpected,"
and so it was, unless
you knew his Irish soul,
and knew that all the weights he lifted,
all the articles and books he wrote,
the dazzling lectures he gave,
were not enough to dispel
the gloom that kept descending.
The good doctors explain the cause
as "bi-polar disorder
aggravated by a change in medication,"
and I'll accept that
because I don't want to know too much
about what goes on inside
as we slog along too far from
Galway Bay, or whatever paradise
he rests in now.

Defying Fate

I really do not want to know
when my time comes for letting go.
I'll grasp and clutch until the end
and each small patch of turf defend.
Hurray for you who graciously
can ease into eternity.
I'll sputter vile obscenities,
denounce life's cruel indignities.
The fates won't get their way with me–
I'll gain God's grace with bribery.

Grump

Should I soon prepare to die?
I resist that–not sure why.
What on earth still holds me here?
Surely not good will and cheer.
Mostly I feel bellicose
or downtrodden and morose,
griping, cross, belligerent,
looking for an argument.
Transcend spite, not sourly slump?
No, I'd rather be a grump.

The Time Has Come?

I gripe about what I can't do–
the things I can are growing few.
'Til recently I still had hope
that somehow I could learn to cope
with life and all the stress it brings,
but now my feeble ego clings
in vain to old and broken dreams,
and as I age it clearly seems
the time has come to gracefully
let go and face eternity.

I've Not Died Yet

I'm glad to note I've not yet died,
a fact my critics have decried.
I take up space, which some resent,
including trolls in government.
Though by my fans I'm idolized
the censors want me vaporized.
On days when I feel vital, stronger,
I plan to stay around much longer.
"Forever young"? That's not for sure,
but for a while I will endure.

Rebel or Fold?

Imprisoned by mundane embodiment,
I constantly proclaim my discontent.
Samsara's chains constrain me night and day
requiring that I must submit, obey.
Rebel or fold? The gods don't give a damn,
and taunt me just to show off that they can.
Can I transcend this tawdry circus show?
A chorus of drunk monkeys hollers, "No!"
but from a duck I'll somehow learn to quack
and ride off free upon a lion's back.

What I'll Do

I have become a vegetable,
a fate I find regrettable.
My soporific stance persists,
all creativity desists,
or else I rant, pontificate,
with fatuous words vociferate.
Creative friends look down on me
and my pathetic poetry.
Here's what I'll do, perhaps next week:
a better medication seek.

Stroke Antidote

I tried to make a clever joke
about the fact I had a stroke,
but I've not made a single one
that turns it into laughs and fun.
In spite of wit there is no doubt
my brief lifespan is running out.
When humor fails is all then lost?
Has some dank Rubicon been crossed?
I'll trudge along another mile,
but sure would welcome fortune's smile.

Hurtling Toward Oblivion

I'm hurtling toward oblivion–
My journey here will soon be done.
The scenery goes racing by
as I approach the day I'll die.
How can I make each moment last?
Why must the days expire so fast?
My dog sleeps quite contentedly,
not craving immortality,
but on I fumble, lurch, and strive,
amazed to find I'm still alive.

Antiquated

A youthful friend purports to be
more antiquated still than me,
but she can think with clarity,
while I get lost in sophistry.
I reign supreme in casuistry
and wallow in senility.
She can converse like an adult
but when I try, the sad result
is verbose, convoluted ranting,
which leaves me speechless, dazed, and panting.

Fighting Anomie

I write these morbid poems frantically,
thus hoping I can fight off anomie.
That does not work, and emptiness pervades,
so I write more, and dwindling life force fades.
Words, words–they never will suffice
to counter death by either fire or ice.
Prepare a space, a still and fertile void,
where nothingness and all can be alloyed.

Improve My Fate

I'm not a brave or social man,
and only do the things I can,
which turn out to be very few,
thus often disappointing you.
I plan to stay in bed all day
and pray my troubles go away.
If they do not, I'll mope and moan,
denounce and curse, protest and groan.
demand the gods improve my fate,
and if they don't, I'll remonstrate.

Loon's Question

My loathsome disability
now makes a flagrant fool of me.
My doddering senility
combines with perfect perfidy.
I trip myself quite frequently
and thus incur much mockery.
My oafish efforts to make jokes
have driven off most decent folks.
Who'll love this lonely, loutish loon?
I hope to get an answer soon.

Where Was I?

Too many friends just age and fade away.
It seems I've lost another one today.
Or maybe she is hiding out from me,
fed up with my deficient empathy.
The IRS absconded with her gelt
but I forgot to ask her how that felt.
The birds convened to decorate her car;
she got herself expelled from Harry's Bar.
But where was I to offer some support?
My schnoz was buried in a glass of port.

Let's Not Wait

I do not like my friends to die
without at least a fond goodbye,
but lately some have taken leave
and left me all alone to grieve.
I'd rather deal communally
with moving to eternity,
so if you plan to soon depart
please take my pleading to your heart.
Let's have a party, celebrate,
and never wait 'til it's too late.

Don't Let Beauty Pass You By

Knowing that you soon will die,
don't let beauty pass you by.
Lilies, pansies, cups of gold–
verdant splendor now behold.
Fondly linger, gaze with thanks
at the rose's regal ranks.
See the wobbly, wondrous fawn
make his way across the lawn.
Years from now when you are gone
still there'll be each day the dawn,
but your eyes will see no more,
what they now can grasp, adore.

Visit Me

My life is very limited these days.
I mope around, lost in a lonely haze.
The gophers will not let me in the yard,
irate that I once made their life too hard.
I like to watch the agile squirrels at play,
but when we talk I don't have much to say.
The ants and their exclusive colony
refrain from any hospitality.
I hardly ever even watch TV,
although I am convinced it's watching me.
I know I'm dull, but still I have a plan:
Come visit me, the soonest that you can.

How I Want to Die

With no great final drama,
here's how I want to die:
Some warm and cozy evening
I'll simply say goodbye,
or fussing in my garden
one cool and rainy day,
the world will hardly notice
that I have slipped away,
The roses still will blossom,
the worms do what they do–
I hope that what I've planted
will bring delight to you.

About the Author

Tom Greening studied psychology at Yale, the University of Vienna, and the University of Michigan, but didn't learn much. Nevertheless, he has practiced psychotherapy in the same office for 50 years. He was Editor of the *Journal of Humanistic Psychology* for 35 years, and that may have affected his sanity. He is a clinical professor at UCLA and Professor Emeritus at Saybrook Graduate School. In college he read too much Chaucer, Pope, and Dryden, thereby becoming addicted to rhyming couplets. One of his narcissistic goals is to upstage Ogden Nash, while still paying tribute to him:

> Cultures may crumble, titans may crash.
> We'll always have Paris, and dear Ogden Nash.

Dr. Greening has published numerous volumes of poetry, including *Words Against the Void* (Revised & Expanded Edition), *Poems For and About Elders* (Revised & Expanded Edition), *Our Last Walk: Using Poetry for Remembering and Grieving Our Pets* (co-edited with Louis Hoffman & Michael Moats), *Nasreddin the Psychologist*, and *Animals I Have Known*.

www.ingramcontent.com/pod-product-compliance
Lightning Source LLC
Chambersburg PA
CBHW050555160426
43199CB00015B/2667